sometimes i fall asleep thinking about you

catarine hancock

central
avenue
publishing

2021

HOW TO BE A POET:
1. rub salt in your wounds
2. watch them bleed
3. call it art

disclaimer
i find poetry
in the most broken things:

crash debris
and shattered glass,
cracked walls
and peeling paint.

i pick letters out
of the wreckage,
try to salvage
something from
all the ruin.

so i make it poetry
and i make it
messy and disjunct
and not always pretty—

not always good—

but always,
always,
me.

always,
always,
every
fucking
piece
of
me.

you come to me in dreams sometimes...

is it pathetic to say i do not wake myself up?

an introduction

dear reader,
a few years ago, i met a boy who lit me on fire.
he reminded me of how warm love could be.

so i closed my eyes to the warning signs
and ignored the damage he inflicted.
i forgot all the lessons i'd already learned.
i stopped knowing better.

dear reader,
a few years ago i met a boy who lit me on fire,
stoked the flames and watched me burn.
i have spent the last four years nursing those wounds.

in many ways, he marked a new beginning for me.
as he destroyed my old self, a new one rose from the ashes,
one that was smarter, braver, and stronger.
smart enough to realize i needed to leave,
brave enough to actually do it,
and strong enough to stay away once i did.
he was the fire to my phoenix.

even still, i've written about our story countless times.
love can be one of the hardest things to shake.
but i have been working towards
saying, "i am putting this down, now,"
and truly meaning it.
i've been waiting for the day
where i could say it was the last time.
i've been waiting for the final poem.

dear reader,
a few years ago i met a boy who lit me on fire
and it took so long to sort through the aftermath.
but now i am healed.
now i am at peace.

now i am ready to finally, *finally*
let him go.

you were in my dreams last night.
you told me, "i read everything you write."
and so i said, "i'm sorry. it's not for you to read.
i didn't write these things to get back at you.
i wrote them for myself."

i woke up with a feeling of closure that evaporated
once i opened my eyes but,
in case you do read everything i write—

i'm sorry. this is not for you to read.
i didn't write these things to get back at you.
i wrote them for myself.

stargazing
i fell in love with you
under the stars.

we'd find the big dipper
while we told each other
about the missing pieces
in our hearts.

you would point at orion's belt
amid telling me about the first time
you fell in love.

i would spot the north star
in between telling you my
deepest secrets.

one of those nights,
you told me,
"i'm just glad i met you."

i looked at you then,
and i didn't know what shone brighter:
the stars or your eyes.

"me too," i said.

funny what a difference a year can make.

i used to try to tell different stories when i wrote:
ones with happy endings,
or ones where it hurt, but eventually, it was okay.
i told stories where everything was so much worse
than anyone could've ever imagined,
or ones where nothing really happened at all.

but now,
no matter what,
the story always comes back to

you.

flatline
i feel our love
like a heart in my hand.

every time the beat falters,
i am afraid it will not start again.

sometimes the blood
pools in my palm,
dripping
down my wrist
like rainwater.

i cannot handle a love
that i have to kick-start
every morning,

i cannot carry that unknown of
will he love me when he wakes up?

when the beat stumbles
i wonder if maybe
it would be better
if it never started again,

if maybe holding a dying thing
is so much worse
than setting down the dead.

your love was a hungry thing.
it never quite understood
that it had already sucked me dry,
that i was always going to come up

empty.

they called us star-crossed lovers.

and maybe that was true.
maybe we were doomed from the start.

but it wasn't the stars that made these wounds.
it wasn't fate that broke this heart.

it was you.
it was all

you.

breaking down
i watched you take a sledgehammer
to our foundation for months
but couldn't figure out why everything
felt so unsteady.
i saw the cracks snaking up the walls
and took too long to connect them to you.

you see, a house is only as strong as its base,
and so is love.

i remember telling you
that what we had built
wasn't as strong as we thought it was,
and you agreed, but what did you do to help fix it?

you were kissing somebody else—
crack—
not speaking to me—
crack—
lying to me about her (and her, and her)—
crack, crack, crack—
until i was standing on a pile of rubble,
staring helplessly at you,
and you were saying,
"i don't know how we got here,"
but how did you not?
how did you not know,
when you were the one
holding the hammer?

and why were you so surprised
when i decided i didn't want to
live there anymore?

who was i?
i would love to be able to remember
who i was before i fell in love.
what did i think it was like?
how did i think it felt?
was i wrong? was i right?

i would love to be able to remember
who i was before you broke my heart.
i think i was less careful, more optimistic,
less likely to fly and more likely to fight.

and that's the part that gets me:
the fact that once, i was more willing to stay,
and i think maybe that was a good thing,
sometimes—not always, but sometimes.

i would love to be able to remember
who i was before you came storming into my life
but all i can recall are glimpses of somebody
who thought they knew heartbreak but really didn't.
not even close. not even a little.

i lost myself in our story. i wrapped myself tight in the happy ending we were supposed to have. it kept me warm when you were nothing but ice.

i said, "we'll be married one day."

i said, "this will all have been worth it."

it took me far too long to realize that all this pain made our happy ending impossible.

yours is the first name
that comes to mind
when i think of how powerful love can be,
even after all this time.
it's like some habit i've yet to break.

but i guess it is true:
you were the definition of a powerful love.

so great i would have done anything to keep it,
so magnificent i forgot myself
entirely.

sometimes i love you really means help me: a rambling
one time, i told you i would love you forever,
and that i would always find it tucked away somewhere
in my heart to forgive you. upon some self-reflection,
i have discovered what might have been unknowingly
hidden in between the lines of that promise:

the saddest thing is that i will love you even like this,
even when it feels more like suffocating,
even when love feels more like a synonym
for denial or being a doormat or
letting somebody hurt you over
and over
and over
again.
i will love you even when you hold me
by the throat.
when you've manipulated me into
letting you choke the self-respect out of me.
i will love you even then
because what else is there to do?
what else do i have left?

i will love you when i am drowning
beneath your hands
and when i am burning
from your matches.
i will love you when i am bleeding
from your snake bites
and when i am bandaging
up the wounds.

because you will be there.
you will always be there
to clean up the mess you've made.
you will never let me down.
you may hurt me every day but you never let me down

not once not ever not ever will you let me down
at least not like that.
you may lie to me and cheat on me and
tell me that i'm crazy and that i told you it was okay
and that i'm the reason you kissed her and then
left her crying i'm the reason you broke her heart
it wasn't because you couldn't control yourself
or have an ounce of loyalty it was because of me
it was all my fault and you may completely rip apart
my sanity and make me believe you are the best
i'll ever have because nobody has ever loved me this much
or at least like this i am so lucky to have somebody
like you love me don't i know how lucky i am and all i do
is keep saying yes and i forgive you and i love you and i think
he doesn't hit me he doesn't hit me at least he doesn't hit me
but if you were here more would you if you were closer
would you hit me if i stood up to you would you hit me if
i left you would you hit me and i think no you would not
even you couldn't find that cruelty inside of you but i still wonder
is this normal to love somebody yet fear every word that comes out
of their mouth is this normal to be perpetually stranded in this in-
between of apologizing or ignoring because i'm either apologizing
for what you did or ignoring it because i love you it's all because i
love you so is this normal to love you even like this is this normal
can somebody tell me if this is what love is supposed to be oh my
god can somebody please tell me if this is fucking

normal?

what made you think loving somebody this way
was an okay thing to do?
what made you think this
wouldn't eventually break me
into pieces?

i never felt more
lost than when
i'd made a home
out of you X

just another moment with you

i loved you
in the fiercest way,
all guttural and snarling,
the way you only love
someone you would die for.

i would have taken a bullet
for you; could you say the same?
would you dive in front of me
when they pulled the trigger?
would you cough up blood
around the words "i love you"?

i asked you once, i did—
would you die for me?
and you said,
would you want me to die?
which was code for
no.

i said,
of course i don't want you to die—
and you took that as your way out
of admitting that you wouldn't,
that it was not like that for you,
that i was not worth a bullet
or a drop of blood.

i know now that a sacrificial love
is hardly love at all,
but that doesn't change the fact that
i would have taken a bullet for you,
and i think i would have taken a bullet for myself,
too, because that is how i loved you—

would you want me to die?

no, my love, my heart, never.

but would you want me to?

LOVE SHOULDN'T FEEL LIKE A PRISON CELL IT SHOULD FEEL FREE
LOVE SHOULDN'T FEEL LIKE A PRISON CELL IT SHOULD FEEL FREE
LOVE SHOULDN'T FEEL LIKE A PRISON CELL IT SHOULD FEEL FREE
LOVE SHOULDN'T FEEL LIKE A PRISON CELL IT SHOULD FEEL FREE
LOVE SHOULDN'T FEEL LIKE A PRISON CELL IT SHOULD FEEL FREE
LOVE SHOULDN'T FEEL LIKE A PRISON CELL IT SHOULD FEEL FREE
LOVE SHOULDN'T FEEL LIKE A PRISON CELL IT SHOULD FEEL FREE
LOVE SHOULDN'T FEEL LIKE A PRISON CELL IT SHOULD FEEL FREE
LOVE SHOULDN'T FEEL LIKE A PRISON CELL IT SHOULD FEEL FREE
LOVE SHOULDN'T FEEL LIKE A PRISON CELL IT SHOULD FEEL FREE
LOVE SHOULDN'T FEEL LIKE A PRISON CELL IT SHOULD FEEL FREE
LOVE SHOULDN'T FEEL LIKE A PRISON CELL IT SHOULD FEEL FREE
LOVE SHOULDN'T FEEL LIKE A PRISON CELL IT SHOULD FEEL FREE
LOVE SHOULDN'T FEEL LIKE A PRISON CELL IT SHOULD FEEL FREE
LOVE SHOULDN'T FEEL LIKE A PRISON CELL IT SHOULD FEEL FREE
LOVE SHOULDN'T FEEL LIKE A PRISON CELL IT SHOULD FEEL FREE
LOVE SHOULDN'T FEEL LIKE A PRISON CELL IT SHOULD FEEL FREE
LOVE SHOULDN'T FEEL LIKE A PRISON CELL IT SHOULD FEEL FREE
LOVE SHOULDN'T FEEL LIKE A PRISON CELL IT SHOULD FEEL FREE
LOVE SHOULDN'T FEEL LIKE A PRISON CELL IT SHOULD FEEL FREE
LOVE SHOULDN'T FEEL LIKE A PRISON CELL IT SHOULD FEEL FREE
LOVE SHOULDN'T FEEL LIKE A PRISON CELL IT SHOULD FEEL FREE
LOVE SHOULDN'T FEEL LIKE A PRISON CELL IT SHOULD FEEL FREE
LOVE SHOULDN'T FEEL LIKE A PRISON CELL IT SHOULD FEEL FREE
LOVE SHOULDN'T FEEL LIKE A PRISON CELL IT SHOULD FEEL FREE
LOVE SHOULDN'T FEEL LIKE A PRISON CELL IT SHOULD FEEL FREE
LOVE SHOULDN'T FEEL LIKE A PRISON CELL IT SHOULD FEEL FREE
LOVE SHOULDN'T FEEL LIKE A PRISON CELL IT SHOULD FEEL FREE
LOVE SHOULDN'T FEEL LIKE A PRISON CELL IT SHOULD FEEL FREE
LOVE SHOULDN'T FEEL LIKE A PRISON CELL IT SHOULD FEEL FREE
LOVE SHOULDN'T FEEL LIKE A PRISON CELL IT SHOULD FEEL FREE
LOVE SHOULDN'T FEEL LIKE A PRISON CELL IT SHOULD FEEL FREE
LOVE SHOULDN'T FEEL LIKE A PRISON CELL IT SHOULD FEEL FREE
LOVE SHOULDN'T FEEL LIKE A PRISON CELL IT SHOULD FEEL FREE
LOVE SHOULDN'T FEEL LIKE A PRISON CELL IT SHOULD FEEL FREE
LOVE SHOULDN'T FEEL LIKE A PRISON CELL IT SHOULD FEEL FREE
LOVE SHOULDN'T FEEL LIKE A PRISON CELL IT SHOULD FEEL FREE
LOVE SHOULDN'T FEEL LIKE A PRISON CELL IT SHOULD FEEL FREE
LOVE SHOULDN'T FEEL LIKE A PRISON CELL IT SHOULD FEEL FREE
LOVE SHOULDN'T FEEL LIKE A PRISON CELL IT SHOULD FEEL FREE
LOVE SHOULDN'T FEEL LIKE A PRISON CELL IT SHOULD FEEL FREE
LOVE SHOULDN'T FEEL LIKE A PRISON CELL IT SHOULD FEEL FREE

i did whatever it took
to keep you calm and happy.
even if it meant
breaking my own heart.
even if it meant
letting you do it for me.

i saw your happiness as my own
so i never had to face the fact
that i didn't really
have any.

cold feet

i was partway out the door for a while, if i'm being honest. i saw the writing on the walls and deep down i knew that they were coming down around us.

i didn't pack all my bags at once. at first it was just a purse, maybe an overnight bag. i would escape for a day or two in the arms of somebody else, or even just for some solitude, but i would always come home. on the walk up to the front door, i was hoping and praying that maybe while i was gone you'd cleaned up the mess you'd made. but it was the same. i thought, maybe if you felt what it would be like to lose me, you'd change.

but you never did change, because while i might've been partway out the door i still had my clothes packed away in the drawers and my books on the shelves. you knew i'd keep coming home. you weren't feeling what it would be like to lose me because you weren't losing me. you never had to beg me to come back.

you didn't need to.

did you really think
my healing would revolve
around your feelings?

i'm putting myself first
this time.

is this what it feels like
to watch a love die,
trapped within cages,
fingers straining but
just out of reach?

is this how it feels
to hold a story
in your hands
but have the pages crumble
when you try to turn them?

how long have i been grieving this, really?
how long have i known this was coming?

when i decided that i was done holding on to nothing, you gave me something to wrap my hands around.

when i decided that i was done putting my time into somebody who didn't have any to spare for me, you suddenly had hours to spend on us.

when i decided that i was done fighting to get you to treat me right, you finally wanted to start trying.

when did we really start to fall apart?
maybe it was in september,
after you ignored me for three days,
and used the line
talking to you just hurts
as an excuse.

it wasn't october, i know,
for that was one of the few months
where you were truly good to me;
you were honest and communicative
and i was so happy to be yours.
i thought the hard part was over.

so perhaps it was in november
when you suggested that
we shouldn't be exclusive,
because *distance is hard*
and i got a sick feeling in my stomach
that i should have listened to.

it could have been in december,
when you lied to my face
about being with other girls
to make me feel bad
for even considering
going on a date with somebody,
casually telling me the truth
only after i'd ruined a friendship
and broken someone's heart.

it could have been in february,
when you kissed another girl
ten minutes after you kissed me goodbye.
at least you told me about that one, i guess.

it could have been in march,

although that was a good month,
when you came to visit and things felt *okay*,
not perfect, not even good, but *okay*.
maybe that was why, though—
it finally hit me that *okay* was not enough.

but then, it could have been in april,
when you kissed her even though
you promised you wouldn't.
you said you *didn't mean it*,
and i still don't know if you were referring to
the promise, or the kiss, or both.

i know now that it was all of these things
that led me to leave you in may,
and there was never a specific moment,
never one thing that broke my heart more
than the rest.

really, it was just the way
loving you wore me down.
whittled me away to the bone,
heart breaking into pieces for you to
keep in your pockets.

intentions

i don't think you intended to hurt me.
at least, not in the beginning.

but once it started, i don't think you felt that bad about it, either.

i've gone over all the options, and that's the one that makes the most sense to me.

you see, it's one of three:

1. you didn't know what you were doing. but that doesn't work because i told you. so that leads me to

2. you knew what you were doing, intentionally or not, but you did nothing to fix it. and there could only be one rational reason why you wouldn't, which is

3. you didn't feel bad about it. you knew what you were doing because i told you, but nothing changed because you didn't care enough. or maybe part of you enjoyed it, but i still won't allow myself to really believe that.

i'm not saying you didn't feel bad at all, just not enough. you apologized and made empty promises and temporary changes, and i do think those were, mostly, genuine attempts. but the will to actually change wasn't inside you. and i believe you realized that rather fast.

that was the problem.

you realized you weren't going to change, and you should have felt bad enough about hurting me to let me go.

but you didn't.

so here we are.

you did not know
how to love me.
and that
would've been okay
if you'd just felt
like learning.

YOUR NAME STILL FEELS LIKE A BULLET
IT'S NOT MY FAULT YOU WON'T PUT DOWN THE GUN
I KNOW

when they say you've grown
some people have told me
you're a kinder person now,
so maybe i should be a little
kinder too.

what they forget
is that i do not know you
now.

i knew you
then.

and the person you were then
was not kind in a lot of ways
and that is the person i loved.
so it doesn't really matter
what you're like now.

i hope, honestly,
that what they say is true.
i hope you're a better person.

for more than just
my own sake.

closure is the one thing i always wanted from you
and you were never able to give it to me.
i've spent years trying to write it into existence.
i think it's what keeps this hole open,
what keeps the poems coming.

i know you follow my instagram
it was a monday when i realized
you were reading my poetry again.
the first thing that went through my head was
"why *wouldn't* he ruin this for me?"

when i sat and i thought about it,
i realized that you probably never stopped.
that nothing i've written about you
has ever been safe.
i guess i knew that on some level,
but it was so easy to ignore
when there wasn't a notification to tell me it was true.
i used to live in a bubble where you only existed
when i felt like thinking about you.
i said anything i wanted without being
afraid of what would happen.

and now that's gone.

i wish i could say that i don't care
and that i'm not scared to write what i feel
but i can't say that and mean it.
the last thing i want is for you to see any of this,
and i do care that you are.
if you read all of the poems you'll know
that i do. it's always there. even at my angriest
i want you to know that it's not for you to see.

but i won't block you.
i won't try to get you to stop.
read it if you want.
maybe you'll learn something from it.

maybe there's something like closure in this.

finally,
i am saying something
and now, after all this time,
you are actually listening.

SELF-REFLECTION:

i wanted us to work so badly because you made me into the worst
version of myself. and i wanted that to be worth it.

i needed it to be.

this is what you don't understand
you didn't have to deal with the aftermath.
you were long gone when i finally realized
what it was exactly that i'd been through.

you didn't have to see me like that,
but everybody else did.

they watched me close in on myself
as i struggled to grapple with the truth.
they helped me as i slowly began
digging up all the red flags
i'd buried along the way.
they loved me through it,
through the fury and the grief
and the confusion and the healing.

they were here. you weren't.

and as much as i can try
to put it into words and explain it to you,
i just can't.

it doesn't matter how long
it takes for you to face the reality
of what happened to you.

it happened.
it was real.
take as long as you need.

there is no time limit, here.

you were supposed
to be my other half—
i am still convincing
myself of all the
reasons you are not.

i hope that,
at the very least,
i am your reminder of what happens
when you treat somebody's love like a game
and play with their heart like it's a toy.

that's all i really want to be:
the face that appears in your mind
whenever you do something shitty.

if i could spare somebody else
from such pain,
that would be enough.

who am i kidding?

i say the poem isn't about you
and then write about a hurricane.
i write about a slow-motion heartbreak,
the gradual cracking of glass before the inevitable shatter.

i say the poem isn't about you
and then rehash the same moments,
play our greatest hits,
almost say your name.

i say the poem isn't about you
but i don't have any other story
to tell.

i say the poem isn't about you
but i wouldn't know how
to tell another story even if i had one.

i say the poem isn't about you
but it is.
it always
is.

SOMETHING HONEST:

every poem i write about you
makes the pain just a little bit more
of a holdable thing,
and i keep hoping
i will be able
to mold it into
whatever i want.

perhaps one day
i could even make us seem

beautiful.

it was all just wrong
i still ask myself:
what if we met now?
would it be different?
would the ending still be the same?

what if
maybe you really were
the right person
at the wrong time?

but i don't think you were.
when it's the right person
at the wrong time,
it's the world that tears you apart.

it's not this.

on the days my ankle still pulses
missing you has changed.
it no longer feels like an anchor
chained around my feet.

nowadays missing you
feels like a fist wrapped around
my throat, sometimes squeezing,
always hovering.
never disappearing.

nowadays missing you
feels less painful
but more permanent,
like an old sprained ankle
that still aches sometimes.
even though it's been
months since i fell.

do you long for me, still?
do i feel like a scar
that didn't heal just right,
like something you can't
forget about yet?
does our end sit uneasily
with you, too?

or is it just the romantic in me
clenching my airway shut
when i look at eyes that
are the same color as yours?
is it just my nostalgia
tugging me down
whenever i hear that song?

missing you has changed.
it no longer feels like an anchor.

it no longer feels out of place.
it just feels ordinary. everyday.
routine.

it feels just like you used to.

don't ask me if i regret you.

ask me if i would do it differently.
ask me if i would have left sooner.
ask me if i have forgiven you.

but don't ask me if i regret you.

i don't think i could even give you an answer.

i am tired
of belonging
to anything
other than
myself

frequently asked questions
why do you still write about it? doesn't that make it worse?

the answer is simple. it's always been simple.

he broke my heart, and i ignored it for a year. i let the wounds sit open and fester and i ignored it. for a *year*. if i had tended to it sooner then maybe i wouldn't be here right now, writing this. but i am. that's my fault. i know it is. but he broke me badly enough that i couldn't even face it at first—how much damage do you think there has to be to cause that? but that's what happened. and that's his fault.

why did you ignore it?

the answer is simple. it's always been simple.

he was supposed to be my soul mate. i thought he was the one. i put my whole being into just the idea of us. it took everything to convince me it wasn't a good one. i had never let anybody treat me like that. before him, nobody got away with what he did. nobody got away with even a mere fraction of it. but he got away with everything. i tried to hold him accountable but it never meant a thing.

he was supposed to be my soul mate. i thought he was the one. the lie was easier to stomach than the truth, until one day, it wasn't.

when did you stop ignoring it?

the answer isn't simple. it's never been simple.

i can't remember when it hit me. maybe it was after i saw him for the first time in months and he apologized. maybe it was before that when he gaslighted me into oblivion. maybe it was when i found out about her. i can't remember when, but i remember how it felt. it felt like drowning and coming up for air all at once.

on the one hand, i was relieved. i felt like a weight had been lifted from my shoulders. it finally clicked that it wasn't really my fault, that maybe i'd had my part but i was not the reason we fell apart.

but on the other hand, i felt like i was being broken all over again. it wasn't my fault but it still happened, and in some ways that made it worse. because if it had been up to me, we would have made it. if it had been up to me, then at the very least we could have been able to fall apart with a little bit more grace.

do you think it will ever completely stop hurting?

the answer is simple. it's always been simple.

no.

for a while,
i found the possibility of another chance
comforting.

that was back when i still believed in us.
i still saw you in my future.
i didn't know how we got from where we were
to our happily ever after,
but i believed it would happen.

and that should've told me all i needed to know.
the reason i had no clue
how we'd get there was because
it wasn't possible.

i always wondered if
there was a universe
where we got it right.

but then i realized...

what if getting it right

is this?

A THOUGHT.

is there a
second chance
somewhere out there
waiting for us?

ANOTHER THOUGHT:

do i want there
to be?

relocate
i'm moving on,
you know,
packing up photos
and silverware
into cardboard boxes
and walking out the door.

he has a place,
and it'll cost less of me
to stay there,
so i unpack my things
and put my clothes
away in the wooden dresser,

but i can't walk to the bathroom
in the middle of the night
without stubbing my toe
on the corner because
i keep forgetting it's there,

i don't know where
he keeps the china
for when company comes over.

i guess you could say
that i feel a little more whole,
but,

there's a part of you
that still feels
like home.

here's a confession:
i know that if you walked through the door and told me you still loved me a part of me would break away and fall into your arms / i know that i would say no but it would sound awfully strange coming out of my mouth / because i never said no even in the end / i always said later / maybe / not right now / but never no / never this is over / i let us fizzle out / let us grow stale like forgotten food in the pantry / i let us wilt until it was too late for water to save us and then i said good / finally i'm free / i dug us up and tossed us into the trash but i left some roots behind so / if you walked through the door today and told me sorry / i love you / let's try again / the pieces of me you broke that i spent so long putting back together would fall like broken glass into your hands / because this is the sad truth / i don't know how to exist in this life and not love you / even just a little / even only in my dreams / i don't know how to look at you and not feel a single thing / even if it's just sadness / or a little regret / or anger / so maybe what i'm trying to say is / please come back / if only so i can tell you no / if only so i can learn how to exist on my own

i had nothing to feel bad about (and you knew it)
i beat myself up over the possibility that i hurt you for months.

i looked at the new boy holding my hand and when the love
swelled up inside of me, the guilt was right there with it, keeping it
company. it took me too long to love him without being afraid.

when i found out about her, the lie you'd kept neatly tucked away,
i felt so foolish. i was furious with myself before i was furious with
you and that just made me angrier—the fact that even still, it was
me who bore the brunt of it, even when i didn't deserve it.

i tried so hard not to love him. i tried so fucking hard. you were
whispering her sweet nothings the whole time, and yet i was
wrong. i was cruel. i was leaving you alone.

maybe i did hurt you, but not in the way i thought i did. it was the
loss of control, and the loss of me with it that hurt you.

it was the realization that i wasn't yours anymore.

and i'll be damned if i ever feel guilty about that again.

cold

i don't know how
to let things go,
so i hold on to grudges
like summer holds
on to september;
i refuse to let you
become something cold.

i know healing should feel
warm and healthy,
not like this;
this feels like i'm letting
something die in my own hands,
this feels like numbness,
like you are
supposed to stay here,
in the back of my mind,
forever.

maybe that is what healing
means for us—
never quite understanding
what this is,
and just becoming okay with
not knowing.
with letting this question sit
on my chest, unanswered,
until one day
i change it from
did he even love me?
to
i don't know if he even loved me
and the fact that it's an unknown
doesn't keep me up at night anymore.

i've resigned myself

to the fact that i will never
be able to get past you
in the way i got over you:
quickly, messily, desperately,
like i would die if i didn't.

i have realized that
letting you go may not
be what's in store for me.
rather, i will hold on tightly,
trying to breathe some type
of life into this, hoping that one day,
it will spit out answers to my questions,
pressing warmth
into something dead to avoid
accepting that maybe

i don't know if he even loved me

was the answer,
the whole point,
all along.

perhaps one day
i will look into the mirror
and not see an empty shell
of somebody who used
to love too much.

but until then,
i stare at my chipped reflection
and wonder when the pieces
will finally stop falling,
or if maybe
i'm slowly shattering
because i find it so easy
to give parts of myself
away.

basically, i did this to myself
here is a cruel piece of irony:
i have spent years trying to press the meaning
out of you.
years trying to flatten you into a clump of memories that no longer
keep me up at night.
years trying to take away your significance.

but in my desire to turn you into nothing
i have made you immortal.

our story sits on bookshelves.
you can find it on google.

i wanted everybody to see you.
i wanted everybody to know.

and for what?

so they knew not to put you
on some pedestal like i did?

foolish me.

my poetry has built you
the highest pedestal
of all.

i let you become
so much more than
you ever deserved
   to be, but i swear
to god, i will not
let you become
      everything

i don't think you would fall in love with the person i am now.
if you did, i don't think i would love you back, at least,
not in the way i loved you before.

there's that question, ringing in the back of my mind:
maybe all we needed was time to grow.

i don't allow myself to think of it for long.
there is no point in believing i will ever
get an answer.

time travel
send me back into the body
of the naïve girl i used to be.
let me look at you with eyes of wonder
once again.

some days, i long to remember
only the good things.
this weight has been so heavy
on my shoulders.

god,
if only we could have been
simple.

you made me feel sorry for being unhappy.
when i stopped feeling sorry for that,
you made me feel sorry for leaving you.
when i stopped feeling sorry for that,
you made me feel sorry for loving him.
when i stopped feeling sorry for that,
you made me feel sorry for finally being happy.

but now?

i am done apologizing.

bloodlust

i think a lot about all the boys i said forever to, handed over my heart on a silver platter and spoon-fed them my arteries. i wonder if they ever think about where it went wrong, where the dinner turned into massacre, where they dug in with tooth and nail, too deep, too hard, too cruel. i wonder if they ever felt sick after. if my blood boiled in their stomachs.

do they read what i write about them? do they know how i painted the end of us? have they read about the bloodshed i made out of their goodbyes? i wonder if they understand why i write so much about them, even in the months and years after.

i would be surprised if they did. it's so easy to put up a front, you know. to smile, tell them i'm doing fine, and turn the five-second conversation into a war between my throat and his fangs when my pen hits the paper. they wouldn't have known my lungs had shriveled. they wouldn't have tasted the blood in my mouth.

i think a lot about the boys i said forever to. i watched them gnaw through me with a smile. now, i like to picture what their hearts might look like on a plate and stab my pen straight through them.

you were my greatest lesson,
but by no means my greatest love.

trust me, i hate writing about you, too
i want you to know this:

when people ask me about you,
i do not speak of you
with the same bloodiness
as my poetry.
if they want to know
my pain, my aching,
they can find it there.

when they ask me about you,
they see a smile,
albeit sad, and rather lonely,
but a smile nonetheless.

i tell them
nothing more
than this:

i loved you,
and you loved me,
but you didn't know
how to do it right.
or maybe you didn't
feel like figuring it out.
either way,
you're gone now.

you are what keeps me
awake on nights where
i feel heavy.
you are the beating heart
of my poetry,
no matter how much
i fight it.

that is why
my words about you
are so bloodstained.

because i have spent
the past four years
trying to fight it.

that works too

it's nights like this when i'm two glasses of wine in and i haven't
had alcohol all summer so it doesn't take long to feel unsteady
/ these are the kinds of nights where all i want to do is tell you i
miss you / but i guess it's that time of year / we met four years ago
around this time do you remember four years ago i was falling
in love with you four years ago i didn't know what was going to
happen four years ago i didn't know i'd still be writing about you

i think about this boy i have now who is so kind and so loving and
does everything right and never lets me go a moment unloved
and i love him so much my entire body shakes with it / and i think
it could've been you / i think it really could've been you but also
could it have been you? / i mean / could it have been you let's be
honest here could you have managed the distance better could
we have tried a little harder could i still be in love with you / yes /
but are you the kind of person to want to do those things? / am i?
/ no we are not although maybe i am 'cause right now i kinda feel
like i'm a little in love with you which is to say i feel kinda sad and
kinda lonely and i keep texting my sweet boy and he keeps telling
me he loves me and i keep fucking crying about it which is to say
right now feels a lot like you haven't quite given up the hands you
once folded around my heart / right now feels a lot like 2015 and
summer and late nights spent staring at the stars and that time you
said you loved me and that time we were invincible and nothing
could stop us until absolutely everything did

here's the fucking truth / i'll write book after book about you
but i'll never say i miss you even though i do i do every day but
especially now especially right now i miss you so much it hurts / i
love him so much i think he might be the one don't you know but i
miss you still / because what else do you do when you stop talking
to the person you loved and it goes radio silent and now you avoid
them like the plague and you get panic attacks when they like a
photo of yours like what else do you do except miss the time when
they felt like part of you and not an invader / things were easier
back then you know / i am so lucky because losing you led me to

him and i am so lucky but i think things were just a little bit easier / not knowing love could hurt like that would have saved me so much time and pain and tears and confusion and it was just easier

so i guess i want to know / do you know the secret to this / do you know the answer / is there a way for me to miss you that will make me less sad? / is there a way for me to miss you that will make it clear i still don't want you here? / even though i do i don't / or is my only option this large aching thing that jumps up and down on my chest whenever i drink too much wine? / because it seems like you're doing fine and i'd like in on the secret

oh / what did you say / did you say you just forgot about it? / forgot about me? / i mean i guess / i guess that works / too i always come back to this:

your mouth, shaped like a promise.
my hands, reaching out to grab it.
you, letting it fall too soon.
me, swiping at thin air.

we were always just too far apart.

i wonder how you remember me.
am i still the soft, flowery girl
you once wrapped around your finger?
or is the space i take up in your mind surrounded
by all the fire and brimstone i have been blasting
at you since you sent my petals up in flames?

you made me
into a forgiving thing.
you turned my heart into
a punching bag,
and i didn't try to stop it.

i watched you
mold me into something smaller
because i thought maybe
at some point you'd realize
you were hurting me.

and you did,
i just didn't know
that was what you'd meant to do.

in a daydream
i have a daydream i like to visit where i tell you all that you did to
hurt me. i lay it out in simple terms. i have a fantasy that involves
me telling you that i hate you until my throat is raw. i like to
imagine that your face drops. that you feel guilty. maybe even a
little sad.

i have a daydream where i get the apology i deserve. i fantasize
about hearing the word "sorry" fall out of your mouth like a rock
because there's finally some fucking weight behind it. i wonder if it
was pride or cruelty that kept it light as a feather.

there are daydreams of mine that convince me you are still a good
person who has done bad things, not the other way around. and
i sit here, always, waiting for you to come back and maybe, just
maybe, make it a reality.

I'VE BEEN
THINKING ABOUT
HOW I MAY NEVER
SEE YOU AGAIN
AND I'VE REALIZED
HOW MUCH I STILL HAVE
LEFT TO SAY

21 things about habits (and you)

1. i don't remember starting to bite my nails; i just know that one day i started and i haven't stopped since. i think that's kind of how our love worked.

2. i could only love you magnificently, with everything in me, or love you not at all. when you had me, you had all of me. there was no compromise. that's probably why it hurt so much to leave you—no fading, no gentle release. just cut, right down the middle. severed clean.

3. when people ask what happened to us, my first instinct is still to explain it in a way that makes it all my fault.

4. they say it takes 21 days to form or break a habit, but it took me exponentially less time to get accustomed to apologizing for you and exponentially more time to stop.

5. 21 days is how long it took you to wrap me entirely around your finger. how fitting.

6. i learned to say "sorry" even when the words should have been coming from your mouth. i said it even when i knew that. i said it even when i told you i wouldn't.

7. it took me around 21 months to figure out just how fucked-up you left me. i buried all of it when i left you. that alone was enough. i let the wounds get infected. dig deeper into my skin. and now i'm stuck with these ugly cuts, watching them slowly scab, and break, and bleed, and scar.

8. i hate writing about you, but like everything else involving you in my life, it is damn near impossible to stop.

9. i miss you, still. it's like an itch i know i'm not allowed to scratch.

10. i don't know if it's okay that i still wonder how you're doing like i really want to know the answer.

11. with time, this will grow stale. even if the wounds remain half-open. somebody else will give me something to write about. i'm sure those words will still reek of you, anyway.

12. you have no clue what you did to me. you never will.

13. i don't even understand what you did to me.

14. i thought this would never happen to me. i thought people might break my heart and for a while, it would ache but then

it would slowly fade and i would get better. i wasn't prepared for this. in all my hopeless romanticism and nostalgic tendencies, i wasn't prepared for this.

15. i have beaten out the habits you instilled in me but a part of me always jumps first to the excuses when somebody wrongs me. jumps straight to the "sorry," ready to fall out of my mouth.

16. maybe i'd rather see the best in people before i see that not everything bad that happens to me is my fault. it's how i love, i think.

17. i still can't believe i managed to walk away from you. it's the bravest thing i've ever done. maybe the most painful, too. but it was right. i was right.

18. i don't think you meant to. i mean, sometimes i do. but at this time, i don't think you meant to.

19. see that? i'll always jump to excuses first. especially for you. almost always for you.

20. i will probably never tell you how i feel. i will never give you any of the honesty found here. i am too kind. i care too much. you still matter to me and i fucking hate it but i will never find that cruelty. you first, as it was. as it will be.

21. i bite my nails until they bleed sometimes. i don't mind the pain. i think that's kind of how our love worked.

this is a confession
sometimes i fall asleep thinking about you
because i want to talk to you
and i can't—won't—do that here
so dreams are my best bet

in my mind
you're so much kinder
so much softer
and you still love me
in a way that makes sense

so sometimes i fall asleep
and open my eyes to find you
smiling at me
and i take your hand
and tell you all the things
i wish i could say:

what my day is like now
where i've been since i last saw you
the songs i've found that i think you'd like

i tell you that there are days
where i still miss you
days where shitty things happen
and i need you because
you always knew exactly what to say

i tell you that i'm sorry too
even if it doesn't feel like i have
anything to apologize for
i'm still sorry

i tell you that i think about how different it would be
if i just hadn't fallen in love with you or
how different it would be

if you hadn't taken my love
and run right off a bridge with it

sometimes i fall asleep thinking about you
so that in my dreams i won't have lost
a best friend and then i wake up
and cry about it because
i feel ashamed to even want
to talk to you at all
when i have such beautiful people
in my life who are so much
better to me than you were

it's been years but i've still got
shit to figure out clearly so
i still cry about you
and i still miss you
and i try not to feel
like a bad person because of it
even though there are times
when i wonder if maybe
you were the love of my life
and everything after
is just trying to fill your shoes but

just because someone left
the biggest wound
that you are still trying to sew shut
just because it keeps reopening
and snapping all the stitches
just because you may let it bleed a little bit
sometimes until it makes you
lightheaded and stumbling
just because you sometimes miss
the people that hurt you
doesn't mean you want them to
come back and

it doesn't mean they should have
never left obviously
because they nearly killed you
obviously they are bad for you
obviously you have done the right thing
in pushing them out of your life but

it does mean that sometimes
you're going to want to text them
and ask them how they've been
and you won't but you'll want to
sometimes you'll wish you could
run into them at the coffee shop
or grocery store so when they ask
what's going on in your life
you could tell them and sometimes
you will even want them back
you will think that this time things
could be different and you would both
do better now even though you still haven't
heard a sincere apology from them
and so sometimes you will fall asleep
thinking about them because in your dreams
they are kind and soft and wise and do everything
right and don't cheat on you or lie to you or
make you feel like you don't deserve to be loved
and in your dreams you can miss them and feel
like it's an okay thing to do and
in your dreams you can even still love them
and it won't seem like something foolish so

sometimes i fall asleep thinking about you
and when you come to me like i thought
you always would i feel a little less broken
and when you ask me how my day has been
i don't feel like i'm lying when i say
better now.

i am still
searching for
you in everything

one time
i compared us to the sun and moon.
our brief encounters were eclipses:
beautiful and over too soon.

perhaps we were
the sun and the moon,
but instead of focusing on
how beautiful our eclipses were,
i should have focused on the way
they were so

dark.

i don't miss you
the same way
anymore

your absence
no longer plagues me

it just sits with me

becoming less of a monster
and more of an old friend

slipping glamour
after i walked away,
i reached out with an offer of friendship
because i loved you and you were,
despite everything,
my best friend.
but you recoiled, pushing me further
and further away.
that was the first time i realized that
this thing between us wasn't so beautiful
anymore.

i put my foot down but i loved you still,
just differently, and it infuriated you.
it was then that it became clear
we weren't so similar, after all.

you did not want a portion
of my time, you wanted all of it.

you did not want my love
if it did not include my body.

you did not want me
if you could not have all of me.

when i was with you,
i was blind to those hard truths.

the second i stepped back from you,
even just a little bit,
everything came into focus.
the shadows lifted.

when i looked into your eyes,
i finally saw the reality of what
you had become.

where i used to see longing,
i saw greed.
where i used to see kindness,
i saw cruelty.
and where i used to see love,
i saw ownership.

i could not recognize a toxic lover yet,
but i could recognize a toxic friend.

when your hold on me faltered,
so did your mask.
and once it slipped,
there was no way for you
to put it back on.

you were
my sun, ☼
☽ moon,
          ✦
     and stars ✦
      ✦
(losing you knocked
me out of orbit)

i was used to crumbs,
because that was all i got from you,
and i always accepted them with a smile.

but the second i stopped giving you everything,
i might as well have given you nothing at all.

only one of us knew what being starved of love
really felt like.

but from the way you acted
nobody would've thought it was me.

WHAT HITS ME AT 2 AM:

you could miss me
and i'll never know it.

after you wished me happy birthday on facebook
sometimes i wish
i was more like
the person i've become
in my poetry.

in my poems,
i am so much angrier
with you than i could
ever be in person.
i hold you hostage
with my words
and make you listen.

in my poems,
i am wounded
but i stand tall
when i see you
and i don't let
you talk down to me.
i walk away.
i am unafraid.

but the person
in my poems
is a dream.

in reality
i still smile kindly
at you.
i am compliant
and quiet
and never make
too much noise
in your direction.
i don't tell you
to leave me alone.

i don't demand
an apology
or an explanation.

i receive your birthday wishes
with a soft smile
and write out a sweet thank-you.
i laugh with you
and ignore the way it makes
my skin feel.

so i guess the reason
i am so angry in my poems
is because for me,
there really is no other
place to put it.
certainly not
in your hands.

envy

if you don't miss me anymore
i don't think i can blame you.

truth is,
i'm just jealous the dull pulse of memory
came for you before it did me.

as if it ever really hurt you in the first place.
as if you ever deserved peace more than me.

i am doing such wonderful things without you.

so why does part of me still wish you were here to experience them with me?

misdirection
this is a poem in which i list all the ways
you could have left me
or i could have left you
that wouldn't have been so ruinous,
a poem where i name all the possibilities and what-ifs
of our entire relationship
and torture myself by remembering every step
it took to get to this one.
somehow, all of these are connected.

1. you grab my hand,
but i am a good person that day.
i do not hold on.
i let you go.
i don't even let myself
get to the point of loving you.
i stop it before it starts,
and i spend the rest of my life
wondering what would have happened
if i had held your hand back
instead of recovering from what happened
because i did.

2. you tell me you love me
and i run.
i do not let the words fall
from my mouth.
i take a second to think realistically.
i consider the chances we actually have.
i say i am sorry, but i can't.
we can't do this. there isn't any point.
i don't get blinded. i don't say we should try.
i break your heart in half, right there.
i spend a lifetime regretting it.
i blame myself for being afraid.
i don't know that i should be thanking

myself for it.

3. you lie to me.
i respect myself enough
to know i don't deserve it.
i refuse to make excuses for you.
i refuse to let you do it again.
the next time you do, i leave.
i do what i should've done,
but didn't have the strength to.
i save myself the second the ship
starts to go down and abandon you.
but i was always so scared of hurting you,
i let myself get hurt instead.
because shouldn't the captain always go down, too?

4. when he gives me a chance
at something good and clean,
i take it.
i don't let you rope me back in
with promises to be better.
i consider everything
we've already been through.
i love myself enough to
not go through any more.
i will rethink the decision
to walk away a thousand times.
it will never seem exactly right.
we weren't doomed, yet.
i will feel bad for leaving when
i didn't think i really had to
(even though i had to).

5. when i find out you kissed her,
i let my own heart break
and then shatter yours too.
i leave. i leave. i leave.

i tell myself this is the reason
i have been looking for.
something big enough to explain
my unhappiness.
i block your number.
i don't let us be friends,
i don't let you still tell me
you love me even when
i start dating somebody else.
i don't let that get into my head.
i don't let us not be finished.
i close the door.
i don't let myself write poems like this.

this is a poem in which i write our story out, again.
i trace the road we traveled and try to pinpoint where
we took the wrong turn, a left instead of a right.
but we started going the wrong way the second i grabbed
your hand back.
we never took a step in the right direction.
you pulled us down a road that i never would've said yes to
had i read the street sign,
one that was all you taking and all me giving.
so i think, what this poem is trying to say, is—
there is no way we could've done this differently.
there is no way we could've done this in a way
that would've actually given us
a chance.

I LONG FOR THE DAY
WHEN YOUR NAME
IS JUST A NAME
AND OUR LOVE
IS JUST A STORY
I CAN TELL WITH A SMILE
OVER DINNER

i still do not believe
you know
how to love someone.

but for her sake,
i hope you are
starting to
figure it out.

forgiveness feels like a double standard
years later and i still
haven't figured out
how to wrap my hands
around my own heart
and accept its mistakes.
i still don't know how
to trust myself.

funny how easy it is
for me to forgive you
for being a storm,
and how hard it is
for me to forgive myself
for loving you through the rain.

THE SUN IS STILL
RISING EVEN THOUGH
YOU ARE GONE.

I AM LEARNING
THAT I MUST TOO.

there is no poetic way
to say this.

i want to be the one
that haunts you.
i want to be
your biggest regret.

some facts about forgetting
1. i still have moments where i see something
and think of what you'd say about it.
i am almost positive that i am always right.
i still know you—or at least, the version of you
that i once held—that well.

2. sometimes, when you waltz into a dream,
it feels like i am waking up for the first time
in months. as if i have been in the dark all along.

3. i still feel like i am coming home
when i see your face. i don't know
how to get that habit to break.

4. i don't think i want to forget, not entirely.
if somebody handed me a pill
that would wipe the memory of us
out of my mind entirely, i don't think i would
choose to swallow it.

5. there's not a rational part of me
that still loves you, but i think my fingertips
still do. they reach in your direction
whenever we find ourselves in the same room.

6. i miss you some days, and i am not afraid
to admit it to myself. it's not the end of the world,
anymore. it's not me being weak. it's less but somehow
more, now, because i know. it's coming.

7. one day i'll see something you would've
found funny and i won't even know it.
i won't even laugh in your place.

THESE ARE THE THINGS WE DON'T TALK ABOUT
after caitlin conlon

the moment our hands touched / how i knew you were bad for me
from the start / the way i ignored it / how i know you're reading
this / and i'm okay with it / the fact that i'm sorry / for this / for
the way i have to remember you / this is for my own sake / how i
never put myself first when it came to you / so now doing that feels
foreign / all the bleeding i had to do before i realized you were the
knife / how you have always been my anchor / how that used to
be a good thing / but now it just means you're keeping me / down
/ the poems i've written / the people that warned me / this gap
between us / the way i used to try so hard to bridge it / the way i
still want to forgive you / the way that i know you would let me

i miss you, still.
despite knowing i shouldn't.
despite knowing it only makes this worse.

I DON'T KNOW HOW
TO LET GO OF
THINGS AND
IT FUCKING KILLS
ME

some thoughts from the hyatt in louisville

missing you comes in waves. i spent a weekend in the place where we once soared, the place that was meant for us. i see you in every floor tile. in the glass reflection of the elevator. do you know it still makes my stomach clench? i have never been good with heights. you held my hand on it, once. you looked at me and smiled and for a moment the only reason my heart was pounding was you. but nothing stays the same. now when i ride the elevator, my friends laugh at how i can't look up. they do not hold my hand. it is a different type of comfort.

missing you comes in waves. it hits me like a tsunami here. only here. today i drown in it. it is the only time where i grieve you in a way that would let you back in should you ask. this is the only time the only feeling i have towards you is sadness, and the anger stays at home. the hatred does not leave its bed.

i love you, here. only here. there are moments where i am sucked into a portal. i feel you, if only for a moment. i do not shove those moments away as quickly as i know i should. but i am not stupid. i am not naïve. i know what happened. i know where i am now. and i do not yearn for you, not in that way.

you could have been the love of my life. i allow myself to sit on that when i am here. i allow myself to think about what it would be like if you had not crumpled me like paper and tossed me aside so many times. i think about where we would be if i had kept letting you. if maybe you would have finally pulled me from the trash and flattened me out, never to ruin me again. if maybe, just maybe, i would have forgiven you.

missing you comes in waves. this was the place that held everything that brought us together. it is now the place that holds everything that destroyed us. you could have been the love of my life. you could have held my hand on glass elevators for the next fifty years. but nothing stays the same. when the elevator lurches and my stomach drops, i ignore the way i can feel your fingertips. i know i will not find your eyes.

when i leave, i remember it. the shine wears off again, and it is simply this: you crumpled me. i loved you until i realized i had to figure out how to unfold on my own.

we used to wax and wane
like the moon.

you would leave
only to return.
we would end
only to begin again.

eventually,
i decided it was easier
to just look up at an empty sky.

i really want to end this, can't you tell?
occasionally i imagine a place where i sit down
and have a conversation with you
and it goes something like this:

you say:
why can't you stop writing about me
isn't it getting kind of old?

and i say:
i just can't
i've tried so many times
you have to believe me

you respond with:
i don't understand why you can't just
get over it

and then i get angry:
of course you don't
you'll never understand it

and then you get angry too:
i've said sorry a thousand times
what else do you want from me?

and then i finally tell you the truth:

honestly, i want you to change majors
so we won't be in the same career
for the rest of our fucking lives
honestly, i kind of wish i'd never have to
see your face again because i really hate it
when we're breathing air in the same room
honestly, i want you to try and take just a damn second
to put yourself in my shoes and think about
what psychological damage getting lied to

and tossed around like dirty clothing
for over a year does to somebody
honestly, i really wish i could let this go
way more than you do because yeah,
maybe it's annoying for you but fuck,
it's so damn horrible for me and
honestly, i say all of this but i don't know
who i am as an artist without you
i don't know who i am as a poet
without the shit you put me through
you make my words worth reading
you make my art worth something
and that just fucking sucks because
honestly, i don't know how to let go
of things and it fucking kills me,
do you finally get it now?
why your apologies don't make
it any better literally at all
because they've barely ever
been anything more than
fucking damage control
and why i have ripped myself
apart over and over again
trying to find something else
to make my writing beautiful
but it's you. it has always been you.
i gave you everything and in some way,
i still am. for some reason,
i still fucking am.

and maybe you say something
and maybe you stay silent.

and maybe i get over it after that

but i probably
don't.

do you really think
i know what forgiveness means?

i am a poet.
the forgiveness begins
when the poems end.

(and they haven't ended yet.)

you were the ink i wrote every word with once.

now the pen is drying up.

and i don't know what to do.

i know if it were up to you,
that this would've been over
a long time ago,
but it's not.

you don't get to tell me
how to heal.

this is the one part of us
that i get to decide.

i am holding onto a
ghost that has long since
decided it no longer
wants to haunt me

who will be the next to break my heart like you did?
what comes after something like this?
surely i have learned enough to know better.
surely i will be able to protect myself.

but i thought the same when i met you,
and yet, look around.

i am not scared of finally being free of you.
i am scared of what comes after i get used
to how that feels.

a quarantine poem
i feel a poem bubbling up in me
and i know
it's going to sound just like
the rest
but i write it

anyway.

i think
there is an alternate universe
out there
where people are free
and we have our lives
and everything is perfect
just like it was before
march

and

i think
maybe in that
alternate universe,
i love you,
and not in the sad, injured way
i know that love to be now,
but in some kind of way
where you did not make me
into someone who keeps
skeletons at her kitchen table.
maybe in that universe
you have been gone
for a long time
but i do not converse
with a ghost in your place.

and then i think

maybe in that
alternate universe,
i don't love you at all,
for i never met you.
maybe in that world
i am not a poet
although i would like to be,
maybe in that world
i do not know how lucky
i am.

or perhaps,
i love you like i used to,
maybe in that universe
you are the one who is different
and i am the same
as i have always been.
maybe that universe holds
the life we used to dream about.

i couldn't tell you
what i'd rather have:

a life like this,
a life with you,
or a life without you at all.

i just know this:

i don't know what life
used to feel like before you.
i only know the after.

and perhaps that is
the only thing anybody knows

now.

i didn't think it would take
this long.

that's part of the reason
seeing the ending in sight
is just as terrifying as it is thrilling—

you have been part of me
for years.

in some ways,
i don't know who i am
if i am not struggling to
move past you.

i don't think you
understand how tired
i am of writing about you.
how _desperately_ i need this
bleeding to stop.

a lesson on handling loss

when they leave you,
hold love as tight
as possible.
it will fight you.
its feet will itch to run
after them.
keep it stitched
to your side.

when they leave you,
force the words
"i am still beautiful"
out of your mouth.
they will brace themselves
against the back of your throat,
drag their claws down your tongue
as you spit them out.
ignore the blood that wells
each time you say them.
speak through the red.
let it drip down your chin.

when they leave you,
do not beg them to stay.
wrap your heart in gauze
and change the bandages
every morning.
they could not do any better.
their hands are clumsy.
you must do this part
on your own.

when they leave you,
do not forget that
you are still here.
even if part of you

went with them,
you are still here.
there are things to be done.
roots to be planted,
blossoms to be nourished,
flowers to be picked.

when they leave you,
keep loving yourself.
you still deserve that kindness.
no matter what,
you deserve that.

if i were given the chance
to do it all over again,
i don't think i would.

i think that if i went into it
knowing the kind of person
you really were,
i would fight so hard to change you
and it would only break my heart more
when i failed.

burn
you were like a sun
to me—
bright and burning
and consuming.

when i touched you
i felt fire shoot down
my arm and i thought,

this must be it,
nothing could be
more than this,

for why would
kissing you
feel like a galaxy
if our love was not
of the stars?

but now i nurse
burn marks
on my hands
from where you
became too much
to hold on to
(that did not stop me),

i replay the memory
of our burnout
and i think to myself,

how glad i am
that you were not
the love of my life.

that does not stop me

from worrying, though.
when your face pops
into my head even now,
i worry.
when i look at something
and am reminded of you,
i worry.

once, it terrified me,
the thought that you
were supposed to be
the one but we were
both too foolish and young
to figure that out,
that we took something great
and reduced it to ash.

i was so afraid
you might have been
the love of my life
and every love after
would simply be trying
to fill the hole
you left in me.

i suppose
there are moments
where that fear still
grips me.

i suppose
there always will be.

learning to be thankful
for the lessons
i learned from loving you
has been the hardest battle
of all.

but i guess,
if it hadn't been you,
if could've been somebody else,
maybe in the future
when i had more to lose.

so if you are
the most painful love
i ever experience,
then i am thankful for that.

ONE DAY I WILL BE PROUD OF WHAT ALL THIS PAIN HAS MADE

a part of me
is always going to
love you.

and
it's the part of me
i hate most about myself.

corpse-watcher
this is not an apology,
but,
you know,
i let us rot after you left
and that was really fucked up.

i watched our love
fall apart and collapse in
on itself
and never buried the body.

i just let it sit for months
and wondered why anybody
would let something so alive
and so beautiful die.

i never wondered why anybody
would decide to not give it
a proper funeral
because i was the one deciding
not to give it a proper funeral.

this is not an apology
by any means
for what i did with the corpse
you left.

you
left me
a corpse.

a shell of something that once beat
and breathed and moved,
a shell of something that once
loved you so much it forgot itself—
i forgot myself.

so yeah,
maybe i should have buried us
when i had the chance to grieve
in a normal way
but the way i loved you wasn't normal
and the way you broke me wasn't either so

i watched a corpse rot
and i can still taste your mouth
and i'm not sorry for this.
i'm not sorry for this.
i'm not sorry for this.

some version of stockholm
i am no longer in a place
that lets me think of you

and that feels
            wrong

i have forgotten how to
blink
breathe
speak
sleep

without first wondering
what you'd say about it

and now i am retraining
myself to just

be

to exist in a way
that does not ask you first

i am no longer in a place
that lets me think of you

and it's
            right

i just don't know what
that feels like
anymore

i am staring at a cracked door
i ask myself,

how many times have i been here,
in this exact spot?

how many times have i stared this moment
in the face?

how many times have i walked away;
how many times have i told myself
i wasn't ready to let this go?

and what has that gotten me?
a two-ton grudge and a mountain of bitterness,
and not one ounce of understanding.
not one sliver of closure.

i ask myself,

was this worth it?
was trying to find an answer that didn't wish to be found
worth it?

i think this time, i'll close the door.

maybe some questions are better left
unanswered.

small-mouthed love

i am not the girl if you want a small-mouthed love. i love big and open, wide and swallowing. you could pluck promises from between my teeth. my heart will crawl out of my throat and fall into your lap. it will curl up there and stay, always coming back no matter how many times you push it off. i am not the girl if you want a quiet love. i love loud and piercing, in permanent ink and maxed-out volume. i leave marks. i am not the girl if you want a temporary love. i am root and stone. dug into the earth. planted. i will stay by you even as i rot and crumble. it is perhaps my greatest strength and my most painful flaw. but still, i remain. and i am yours for the taking, love. but only if you know what it is you're getting into. only if you understand that should you love me, it is not a choice you can so easily take back.

I BELIEVE IN LOVING LOUDLY / IN HUGGING YOU
OBNOXIOUSLY IN PUBLIC / IN KISSING YOU GOODBYE
IN FRONT OF YOUR PARENTS / IN KISSING YOU IN
FRONT OF YOUR PARENTS JUST BECAUSE I FEEL
LIKE IT / IN SITTING ON YOUR LAP AT PARTIES / IN
SLOPPINESS / IN UNAPOLOGETIC AFFECTION / IN
MASSIVE DECLARATIONS / I BELIEVE IN LOVING LOUDLY
/ WITHOUT SHAME / WHAT GOOD IS IT ANYWAY / IF IT
ISN'T SOMETHING YOU CAN YELL ABOUT

adaptation

losing you felt like
a forest being thrown
into drought,
like i had been cut off
from everything i needed
to survive.

it was like when the air
is so hot and dry
and you swallow but can't seem
to fill your lungs.
i was suffocating
on your absence.

i felt myself wilt
and wither and crack,
a hardening that took
the longest time to finish.

for so long i was afraid
to breathe deeply.
i did not think
there would be anything
there waiting for me.

but over time i grew
from forest to scorched earth,
from lush and green
to hard and sand.
i was beautiful
in a new, different way.
eventually,
i stopped longing
for my canopies
and started loving
my deserts.

now, the air is no longer
thick with your rain.
instead,
it is hot with my sun.

this is what i'm waiting for:

one day,
i am going to see you again.

and for the first time,
it isn't going to matter.

i am slowly
rebuilding myself
into the person i was before:

somebody bright,
somebody happy,

and,
most importantly,
somebody who doesn't
need
you.

this pain will fade
and i will learn to become
something without you

just you wait—

i am going to become
the greatest thing
in your absence

sleep paralysis

one time, i loved a boy who seemed to write me into existence. i don't mean that i wasn't anything before him—i was. but i think i was small. i think i didn't know somebody could look at me like that, and after i figured it out i didn't think anybody else would look at me like that again. that was almost ten years ago. the person i was then feels so far away now but at the same time if i reached out i could brush her cheek with my fingertips. if i could, i would tell her, *you sweet, foolish girl, you have no idea what's coming. one day you won't even remember the sound of his voice, much less how it felt to love him.*

if falling in love for the first time is like a sweet dream then experiencing your first heartbreak is like sleep paralysis. we—the love we had—became the phantom crouched at the foot of my bed, and i was stuck, forced to watch the moment it all came crashing down again and again. eventually, i could move my fingertips underneath the covers. eventually, the phantom faded from view. i woke up. stopped loving him. moved on.

in many ways, love still feels like a dream and losing it still feels like i'm pinned to my bed by something invisible, with no choice but to relive those final moments over and over again, staring into the eyes of the person who now holds my crumpled heart in their fist. but now, love is a dream that i know i could wake up from any moment. i still float through it but i'm not as surprised when the alarm clock rings. i've grown to understand that it always rings exactly when it's supposed to. and as far as heartbreak goes, i still haven't figured out how to make those initial moments any less terrifying and painful. i don't think i ever will. but i don't let myself get trapped there anymore. i know how to breathe, how to slowly wiggle my toes, then my ankles, then my legs. i know how to set myself free. the ghost at the end of my bed is a lesson, not a nightmare. it always has been. i've just been too scared to realize it.

one time, i loved a boy who tried to erase every part of me and recreate me to his liking. i've spent a long time fixing the mess he left. i made myself into somebody the old me probably wouldn't even recognize. that was almost five years ago. the person i was then feels almost further away than the person i was five years before that. i don't think i could find her no matter how far i reached. i don't even know what i would tell her—*one day you won't even remember the sound of his voice*? i couldn't say that. it would be a lie.

when that dream, if you could call it that, finally ended, and the phantom appeared—that was the only time i welcomed it. i watched the end of us and i didn't flinch. i said, *i was right. this was the right thing to do*. i said, *i needed to wake up*.

i said, *you may be scary but you can't hurt me here.*

i would've bloomed regardless
you can tell people
that you made me
into who i am today,

that you molded me
with your own two hands,

that my being bears
your signature.

but the truth
is that i always knew
i was destined for greatness.

i didn't need
you to break me
to trigger some
great transformation.

you see,
before you came along,
i knew i was beautiful.

and i may have lost that
for a moment,
but after you left,
i still knew
i was beautiful.

nothing you did
could have ever
changed that.

i haven't thought of you in days
it's been three weeks
and it's the longest i've gone in nearly four years
without writing a poem about you.

well,
it's more like it's been three weeks
and it's the longest i've gone in nearly four years
without *needing* to write a poem about you.

because even when i couldn't find the words
the urge was always still there,
bubbling up in me like a soda can
that's been knocked around
one too many times.

i guess
this poem kind of
cancels out what i just said but,
i mean,
isn't a poem about how i don't feel the need
to write poems about you
better than yet another poem in which
i repeat the same battered lines
and open the same old wounds
because i can't figure out how
to forgive you or let it go or whatever,

but,
maybe this is forgiving you?
maybe this is letting it go?
the fact that i have to force you
to come to mind rather than
everything else having to fight
their way into your spotlight?

i don't know if this will last

but i like this feeling of peace
and it's the first time in a long time
that i don't give a shit what you're up to
and it's the weirdest damn thing
in the world.
it feels so strange in my hands.

i think i'm starting to forgive you.
maybe it's the new decade or maybe it's just time
but i think it's finally happening.
maybe tomorrow i'll wake up and feel the same
as i have for so long but i think right now,
if only for a moment, i mean it when i say

i'm good. i'm fine.

and i hope you're the same.

for a while, the only thing i felt
when it came to you was sadness.

then slowly, over some months,
that morphed into anger.

eventually, it was both:
sadness and anger,
grief and rage,
agony and fury.
it stayed that way for a long time.

and now, finally,
the only thing i feel
when it comes to you
is nothing.

i think many would call it
peace.

once, i grieved the way
i was not enough for you.

now, i am so thankful,
thankful that other
forces were looking
out for me when
i was not.

ghosts

sometimes, people haunt you, and the best thing you can do is let them. when you wake up in the morning and their ghost greets you by the coffee maker, where the real them always used to stand, give them a smile, offer them a cup. it's okay to find peace in the presence of a phantom. somebody who used to be such a solid figure in your life is so faded you could pass a hand through them. it's okay to grieve that fact. it's okay to seek out the places and the things that remind you of them—bookstores, cafés, park benches—if it helps you understand what absence feels like. if it helps you learn how to enjoy those things without them. when people haunt you, you can't always close your eyes and have them be gone when you open them again. you can't wish them away. sometimes, you just have to let them stick around, for as long as you really need them to. even if you don't know it. until you can go to the coffee maker and not see them standing there, until you can go to the bookstore and it still holds that magic that it once had, until the roses smell just as sweet as they used to, until you no longer wish them away each night, until they fade on their own, and you don't even notice.

growing pains
i hope you understand now.
i hope you understand that in a lot of ways—
in most ways—
this stopped being about you
a long time ago.

sure,
if somebody dug under the surface
of these poems,
they'd find you there,
but you are no longer the root of this.
if they kept digging,
they'd find me—
not you, not us—
just me,
at the center.

you changed me.

you changed me
while you were here
and you've continued
to change me in the years
you've been gone.

it has taken me a long time
to realize that those changes
were for the better.

threadbare

i used to believe we were soul mates,
but i don't think our souls
would even recognize each other anymore.

the last time i looked into your eyes
i could already feel the ends
of the string that tied us together
fraying and breaking away.

i think if i looked into them now,
only a few limp threads would remain,
weak and powerless,
signifying nothing other than
an old and long-lost connection.

how amazing it feels
to be free of you.

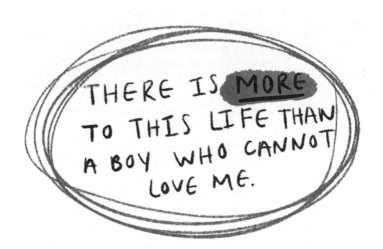

i have learned that sometimes
the best thing to do is listen to your scars.

the worst heartbreaks stay with you for years
but they protect you the whole time.

the biggest wounds may take the longest
to heal but also have the most to learn from.

your past is not always the enemy.
sometimes, it can be your greatest friend.

if you made it this far

three years ago i wrote a book and at the end of it i said it was over, that i had forgiven you. a few months later i saw you and realized, immediately, that it wasn't. there were wounds not yet closed, truths i had yet to grapple with. i just wasn't over it yet, no matter how badly i wanted to be. and i hope you know by now that i really wanted to be.

two years ago i wrote another book and i told you i was done writing about this, that it was doing more harm than good. i was hurting myself for the sake of my art, i said. well, that book came out and soon after it dawned on me that while it hurt to write about you, it hurt even more to push the words back down. so i let them out. and now, here i am. finally coming up empty. after all this time.

i can tell you now with certainty that this book does not contain the same false promises as the others. i will not promise you that i'll never write another poem about you again. i will. i will write dozens more. but it won't be the same. they won't be raw, like they've been for the past five years. they'll be reflective, maybe a little sad, and sometimes they'll hold that anger that's buried within every syllable of this book, but they just won't be the same.

i also won't say i've forgiven you entirely. i've forgiven you enough. you have received all the forgiveness i can muster. i will never be able to completely forgive you because i will never completely understand why you acted the way you did. i have made peace with what i can and stopped ruminating over what i can't.

i spent a long time wanting someone to treat you the way you treated me, but all i want now is to be done with this. i'm just tired. so i'm done. this is done, now. you can be as happy about it as you want. i'm happy, too. this chapter of my life is over.

i'm finally closing the door.

THE MOMENT OF CLARITY I'D BEEN WAITING FIVE YEARS FOR:

i guess you could say i just simply don't have the desire to tell our story anymore. it happened. and it killed me. it killed me for years. and now i'm looking forward without you lurking behind me for the first time since it started. i just don't feel the need to keep rehashing it. i'm finally away from your shadow and the light feels fucking amazing.

and you? well, you're wherever you are, doing whatever you're doing, and i have finally stopped caring. i have stopped caring about whether or not you think about me anymore, and i have stopped caring that many signs point to "yes." i have stopped caring about some final conversation that will make any of this make sense; i've stopped caring about how that will never happen. i have stopped caring if you're reading this and i have stopped caring about how it makes you feel if you are.

it's been too long since i've tasted peace. but it's here now and i don't plan on forgetting its flavor anytime soon.

to you, reader:

there are times when people just leave. hearts just break. love just dies. wounds just bleed. but time presses on. new people arrive. hearts begin to beat again. a better love takes root. wounds finally heal. if you are hurting, let time work its magic. it is slow for a reason. this waiting is a kindness. let it hold you. relish that feeling of becoming new. feel your heart beating strongly in your chest. it is another day. another chance. open your eyes, and step into the sun.

i am beginning to adjust
to a life without you in it—
and i am realizing that it can,
indeed, be beautiful.

acknowledgements

there are so many people i want to thank for the parts they've played in making my dreams as a writer come true that i'll probably forget some. if you don't find your name here, just know that i am still forever grateful.

to michelle at central avenue, thank you so much for taking a chance on me. i don't think i will ever be able to fully express how thankful i am.

to mom and dad, grandmom, and ga and pa, i'm sorry i kept this part of my life secret for so long. i'm glad you're a part of it now. i couldn't ask for a more supportive family, not just for my writing, but for everything i do. thank you for teaching me to be kind, smart, and passionate.

to harrison, i'm glad i have a little brother who is cool enough to be proud that his sister writes poetry instead of embarrassed by it. i'm also glad that i have a little brother who is also one of my best friends.

to ashley, kason, catherine, and all of my friends at school, when i came into college i did not expect to be met with such support because i did not receive a lot of it in high school. when i decided to start talking about my writing and self-publish my first collection during fall of freshman year, i was blown away by how many of you not only congratulated and encouraged me, but also bought the book. you all helped me become shamelessly proud of my art. ashley, thanks for being the best roommate a girl could ask for, who drove me to see *shades of lovers* in-store the day it came out after a full day of classes despite it being all the way across town. kason, spending time with you was often my favorite way to pass time in high school and it still is now. thank you for being my person to rant to about anything under the sun and for sticking by me for the last eight years. catherine, you are one of the most kind, genuine people i know and i am so glad we've had the chance to create so many fun memories together. i know whenever i feel down i can just come to you.

to bethany, you were the one person in high school i felt completely comfortable talking about my writing with and to this day i know i can turn to you when coming up with a new book idea or working through a creative block. but more than that, you are one of my best friends and confidants. thank you.

to blake, thank you for supporting me unconditionally. i am so grateful for the love we have shared. i have grown so much by your side and i cherish every single memory. thank you for being my best friend, my favorite person, my emerald green.

to all the teachers i have had over the years—deborah sogin, ryan marsh, dr. mark kano, dr. angelique clay, nan mcswain, dr. hetzel, dr. johnson, beth wilson, chelsea bugg, and so many more—thank you, from the bottom of my heart, for all that you have taught me. i would not be who i am today without you. though many of you were or are my voice teachers or choral directors, you've also had an impact on who i am as a writer. you encouraged me to be myself, to love life unabashedly, to chase my dreams. you have also been some of my biggest fans since i started writing books and i know that you will always be in my corner, cheering me on, wherever life takes me.

to trista mateer, amanda lovelace, cyrus parker, zane frederick, caitlin conlon and the wonderful poetry community, i have looked up to so many of you for such a long time, and the fact that i can call many of you a friend now is still a surreal feeling. thank you for welcoming a young 18-year-old girl with open arms in 2017 and for providing your advice, support, and friendship ever since. special thank-you to trista for editing this book and being an amazing mentor and friend.

to caroline, signe, jaden, emily, samia, ashton, grace, lauren, and sarah, you guys are my original poet family. we've built a bond that only comes with reading each other's angsty (and sometimes bad) poetry when we were teenagers. and now we're all grown up. i know some of you don't write anymore, or as much, but you'll always be poets to me. i'm so glad we still keep in touch.

and finally, to all of my readers, thank you. thank you, thank you, thank you. it doesn't matter if you've been reading my work since i was thirteen or if this book was your first time; thank you. i never could have expected to reach so many people with my writing. when i first started writing, i thought just a few hundred people would enjoy it enough to follow me. i never thought i would have an audience of a few hundred thousand. you have changed my life in so many ways. it is perhaps my greatest joy to create art that has helped you smile, laugh, grieve, and heal. here's to the past seven years, and the many more to come. i love you.

about the author

Catarine Hancock is a 21-year-old Kentucky native. She has garnered an audience of over 200,000 on social media in the past six years she has been sharing her work online. Catarine writes predominantly about love and its many aspects, both the good and the bad, as well as political topics that are dear to her heart, such as feminism and gun control. She is an activist, college student, and opera singer as well as a writer, and attends the University of Kentucky as a Vocal Performance major. Her first two collections, *the boys i've loved and the end of the world* (2017) and *how the words come* (2018) are no longer in print but can be read for free on her Wattpad. Her third collection, *shades of lovers* (2020), can be bought wherever books are sold.

You can keep up with Catarine on her social media platforms:

Instagram: @catarinehancock
TikTok: @catarinehancock
Wattpad: catarinehancock
Tumblr: catarinehancock
Twitter: @writingbych
Pinterest: Catarine Hancock
Facebook: Catarine Hancock

Published by Central Avenue Publishing, an imprint of Central Avenue Marketing Ltd.
www.centralavenuepublishing.com

SOMETIMES I FALL ASLEEP THINKING ABOUT YOU

Trade Paperback: 978-1-77168-234-3
Epub: 978-1-77168-235-0
Mobi: 978-1-77168-236-7

Published in Canada
Printed in United States of America

1. POETRY / Love   2. POETRY / Women Authors

10 9 8 7 6 5 4 3 2 1